Merton Leland Miller

A preliminary study of the pueblo of Taos, New Mexico

Merton Leland Miller

A preliminary study of the pueblo of Taos, New Mexico

ISBN/EAN: 9783337729127

Printed in Europe, USA, Canada, Australia, Japan

Cover: Foto ©Suzi / pixelio.de

More available books at **www.hansebooks.com**

The University of Chicago
FOUNDED BY JOHN D. ROCKEFELLER

A PRELIMINARY STUDY

OF

THE PUEBLO OF TAOS

NEW MEXICO

A DISSERTATION SUBMITTED TO THE FACULTIES OF THE GRADUATE
SCHOOLS OF ARTS, LITERATURE, AND SCIENCE, IN CANDIDACY
FOR THE DEGREE OF DOCTOR OF PHILOSOPHY

DEPARTMENT OF ANTHROPOLOGY

BY

MERTON LELAND MILLER

CHICAGO
The University of Chicago Press
1898

ANALYSIS OF CONTENTS.

3

PREFATORY NOTE.

This brief account of the Pueblo of Taos is the result mainly of a three-months' visit at the Pueblo in the summer of 1896. Now that a few friends have been made there, it is hoped that at a later time a more complete and thorough study may be made.

The repeated references to the *Papers of the Archæological Institute of America* show how much I am indebted to the writings of Mr. A. F. Bandelier.

In spelling the few native names which occur in this study and which I have not seen mentioned before, I have followed the alphabet given in Powell's *Introduction to the Study of Indian Languages.*

M. L. M.

A PRELIMINARY STUDY OF THE PUEBLO OF TAOS, NEW MEXICO.

One of the most attractive valleys in New Mexico is that of Taos. It is situated in the center of the northern part of the territory, not many miles from the Colorado line. Shut in by the Taos range of the Rocky mountains on the east and by the mesas which border the Rio Grande on the west, it is today, as it has been in the past, one of the best watered, greenest, and most fertile valleys in the Southwest. The one thing above all others needed in New Mexico is water. Taos valley, while it has not an over-abundant supply, has enough to enable the people to irrigate as much as they wish, except in unusually dry seasons. The several streams which water the valley, the principal of which are Lucerro, Pueblo, Taos, and Fernandez creeks, are rarely entirely dry, unless the water is turned aside into the acequias, the large irrigating ditches which run from every stream. Perhaps no crops, excepting maize, the staple Indian product, could be raised without irrigation. " Corn may grow on elevated table mountains or plateaus that are hundreds, nay thousands, of feet above a spring or brook." [1] Under such circumstances the water must be economically used, and often in midsummer, when the snow on the mountains has melted, must be used continuously day and night, as the supply is not large enough to permit many to irrigate at the same time.

The valley owes its fertility and attractiveness in large part to its altitude and its location in the mountains, whose melting snows supply the streams. Its elevation is over 7,000 feet. In the summer days, when the sun shines, as it does during the greater part of the warmer season, it is very hot, but the air is so dry that one does not seriously feel the heat ; and as soon as the sun sets the air is very cool and refreshing, often, after a very hot day, even chilly.

The report of the first geological survey of this region contains a notice which is interesting because it helps to show how attractive Taos valley has appeared to everyone who has seen it, not merely as compared with other less favored parts of New Mexico, but when com-

[1] *Papers of the Archæological Institute of America*, American Series, III, p. 156.

pared with other regions better supplied with water. "The Taos Basin has, perhaps, a larger amount of tillable land in one compact body than is to be found similarly situated in any other part of the area. The soil is admirable, being derived from the Archæan and Carboniferous with no small admixture of volcanic material; while at but a few inches below the surface is a tufaceous limestone, which cannot fail to be a constant amendment to the soil. Water is supplied by large streams — Pueblo, Ferdinand, and Frijole creeks. A population of not far from 10,000 inhabits this basin, and yet a large part of the land is still wild." [1]

Mr. Poore, in his report, contained in a Census Bulletin on the Pueblo Indians, says : " It would be difficult to find in the west, where farming is dependent upon irrigation, a more desirable tract of land than that owned by these Indians. The water, carried in subwaterways, or acequias, commands a large portion of the reservation." [2]

Eight or ten miles west of the valley flows the Rio Grande. As one looks westward he sees only the low line of the mesas and many miles farther, though it seems but few, the irregular outline of the distant ranges of the Rocky mountains. No sign of the Rio Grande flowing between its cañon walls can be seen. Far to the south rise the nearer, but still distant, heights of the Mora range, beyond which lies the city of Santa Fé. To the north stretches the gently sloping mesa as far as the eye can see, rising gradually toward the east and merging into the foothills of the Taos range. This valley, which the American and the Mexican find so attractive, the Indian had discovered and occupied before the white man came. Toward its northern end and close to the foothills on the eastern side, under the very shadow of the towering Taos peak, the Spaniards, when they first visited the country, found the Indian pueblo of Taos, or Te-uat-ha,[3] as it was called in the native idiom. Taos was then, as it is today, the most northerly of the pueblos and has, perhaps, the best location.

The account of the first visit of the Spaniards to Taos, as given by Castañeda, presents a difficulty which it may be well to state even if

---

[1] "U. S. Geographical Survey West of 100th Meridian," III, Supplement : *Geology*, pp. 364–5.

[2] " Eleventh Census of the U. S., Extra Census Bulletin," *Moqui Pueblo Indians of Arizona and Pueblo Indians of New Mexico*, p. 100.

[3] *Papers Arch. Inst. of Amer.*, III, p. 123. Bandelier states that the name Taos is corrupted from the Tehua word Ta-ui, *The Gilded Man*, p. 149, footnote.

no light be thrown on the matter. In 1540 Coronado had set out from Mexico for the north and particularly to search for the rich and popular city of Quivira, of which he had heard. After he and his company had reached Cibola (Zuñi), Hernando d'Alvarado was sent on ahead with twenty men to accompany certain Indians who had come from villages to the east to see the strangers. Alvarado was to return in eighty days. "Alvarado partit donc avec eux. Cinq jours après ils arrivèrent à un village nommé Acuco, qui est construit sur un rocher. Les habitants qui peuvent mettre sur pied environ deux cents guerriers sont des brigands redoutés dans toute la province. . . . . A trois journées de là, Alvarado et les siens arrivèrent dans une province que l'on nomme Tiguex. . . . . A cinq journées de là, Alvarado arriva à Cicuyé, village très-fortifié, et dont les maisons ont quatre étages."[1]

When Don Tristan d'Arellano reached Cibola with the rest of the army, Coronado ordered him to allow the army a rest of twenty days and then to follow the road which he himself was about to take to Tiguex. At Tiguex Coronado found Alvarado awaiting him. Later they were joined by Arellano with the army. Some time was spent here till, finally, the people rose in revolt because of the excessive demands made upon them by the soldiers. While the siege of Tiguex was in progress, Coronado went on to Cicuyé and from this latter point set out on his long march to the northeast. When he had been on his way for some days, provisions began to run short, so the army was sent back under command of Arellano, and Coronado went on with only a few men.

In July or late in June, 1541, Arellano reached Tiguex on his return march. He then "donna ordre au capitaine Francisco de Barrio-Nuevo de remonter le fleuve avec quelques soldats, dans la direction du nord. Cet officier visita deux provinces : l'une se nommait Hemes, et renfermait sept villages ; l'autre Yuque-Yunque." The inhabitants of Yuque-Yunque " se retirèrent dans les montagnes, où ils en avaient quatre autres fortifiés, dans une situation très-difficile : l'on ne pouvait y parvenir avec les chevaux. . . . . A vingt lieues plus loin, en remontant la rivière, il y avait un grand et puissant village que l'on nommait Braba, les nôtres lui donnèrent le nom de Valladolid. Il était bâti sur les deux rives du fleuve, que l'on traversait sur les ponts construits en madriers de pins, très-bien équarris. L'on vit dans ce village les étuves

[1] " Relation du Voyage de Cibola par Pédro de Castañeda de Nagera." II. Ternaux-Compans, *Voyage de Cibola*, pp. 69-71.

les plus grandes et les plus extraordinaires de tout le pays. Elles étaient soutenues par douze pilliers, dont chacun avait deux brasses de tour et deux toises de haut. Le capitaine Hernando d'Alvarado avait déjà visité ce village en allant à la découverte de Cicuyé. La contrée est fort élevée et très-froide ; la rivière qui l'arrose est fort profonde et rapide, et on n'y trouve pas de gué. De là, le capitaine Barrio-Nuevo revint au camp, après avoir laissé tout le pays parfaitement tranquille."[1]

In the identification of the villages mentioned in this account of Castañeda there is some difference of opinion. Cibola, it is generally agreed, is Zuñi. Acuco, it is also generally agreed, is Acoma. Tiguex has been located by Mr. W. W. H. Davis on the Rio Puerco, which joins the Rio Grande near the present town of La Joya.[2] Mr. Simpson places it " on the Rio Grande, below the Rio Puerco, at the foot of the Socorro mountains."[3] Mr. Bandelier believes it was near the site of the modern Bernalillo on the Rio Grande. Mr. Simpson and Mr. Bandelier both place Cicuyé at Pecos, while Mr. Davis places it on the Rio Grande, "somewhere in the valley of the Guadalupe, and but a few miles from its mouth."[4] Now, it will be noticed that Alvarado, in his march from Cibola to Cicuyé, traveled from Cibola to Acoma in five days, from Acoma to Tiguex in three days, and from Tiguex to Cicuyé in five days more. But if Tiguex and Cicuyé were at any one of the places which have been suggested, and if the Braba mentioned by Castañeda were situated where Taos is today, it is difficult to see how Alvarado could have reached Cicuyé in the time he did, if he went so far north as Taos, which is over sixty miles in a direct line north of Pecos. It is further hard to understand how he could have reached Taos without having seen or heard of the Tehua pueblos of Tesuque, Nambé, Pojuaque, San Ildefonso, Santa Clara, and San Juan. If these identical villages did not exist then, there were, nevertheless, Tehua Indians in the same general region. Again, the river which waters Taos valley is referred to as very deep and rapid, and as having no fords. In the whole valley today there is no stream which will answer this description, nor is it easy to suppose that

---

[1] II. Ternaux-Compans, *Voyage de Cibola*, pp. 137-9.

[2] W. W. II. Davis, *The Spanish Conquest of New Mexico*, p. 185, note 1.

[3] General Simpson, "Coronado's March," Smithsonian Report, 1869, p. 335.

[4] *Papers Arch. Inst. of Amer.*, I, p. 17. Davis, *The Spanish Conquest of New Mexico*, p. 198, note 1.

the streams which now water the valley were once so deep that they could not be forded. Today one can ford any of the streams at almost any point on foot. The reference may be to the Rio Grande, though it certainly does not water that part of the valley in which Taos pueblo is situated. And yet Mr. Bandelier says of the identity of Braba and Taos "it is unmistakable."[1] Certainly the description of the village as being built upon the two banks of a stream which one could cross on bridges made of well-squared timbers is in exact accord with the conditions at Taos today. I find no reference in Mr. Bandelier's reports to Alvarado's visit to Taos, but Mr. Davis says, "Up to the point where the army was left upon the plains, the Spaniards had passed through the following provinces, which are given in the words of Castañeda."[2] Then follows the list, which includes "Valladolid or Braba," and ends with the statement, "Tiguex is the central point, and Valladolid the last toward the North-east."

This question of location is apart from the other question, whether the people are today living in the same buildings which the Spaniards saw. Mr. Bandelier positively says: "With the exception of Acoma, there is not a single pueblo standing where it was at the time of Coronado, or even sixty years later, when Juan de Oñate accomplished the peaceable reduction of the New Mexican village Indians."[3]

It is not particularly significant in this connection, but it may be noted that at Taos, only a few rods east from the present houses, are the ruins of older buildings. They are little more than a heap of earth and loose stones, but one can occasionally find a very distinct fragment of an old wall built of adobe bricks of a different form from those now made by the Taos people. The people themselves say, and it is undoubtedly true, that in the old days adobe bricks were not made, but a wall was built by laying one layer of mud on another, and simply allowing time for each layer to dry. They further say that not long

[1] *Papers Arch. Inst. of Amer.*, I, p. 23, footnote.

[2] *The Spanish Conquest of New Mexico*, p. 221.

[3] *Papers Arch. Inst. of Amer.*, III, p. 34.

I do not know what Mr. Bandelier's authority is for making this statement, but, in view of the well-known fact that the pueblo peoples have so often moved their towns, it seems safe enough without evidence to the contrary to hold this view. I notice that Mr. Prince says: "In several instances, as at Taos and in the western pueblos, the people are now living in identically the same houses which were then (when Columbus discovered America) occupied."—L. B. Prince, *Historical Sketches of New Mexico*, p. 31.

ago there were other ruins just across the little stream. So it may easily be that these ruins, to which the people still point as their former homes, situated with reference to the creek just as are the houses of today, are what is left of the houses which the Spaniards saw.

Taos appears several times prominently in opposition to the Spaniards. Possibly its position farther from Spanish influence, or the necessity which the people were under of defending themselves from their enemies, enabled it to maintain its independence more effectively than the villages farther south.

Some time after 1650 a conspiracy was formed at Taos and spread as far as Moqui. I quote from Bandelier: "Y despues de algun tempo despacharon del pueblo de Taos dos gamuzas con algunas pinturas por los pueblos de la custodia, con señales de conjuracion á su modo, para convocar la gente á nuevo alzamiento, y que dichas gamuzas pasaron hasta la provincia de Moqui donde no quisieron admitirlos, y ceso el pacto por entonces."[1] Although Po-pe, the instigator of the great conspiracy of 1680, was an Indian of San Juan, he seems to have made his plans at Taos and to have received much assistance from the people there. Certain it is that they were among the last to submit to de Vargas at the time of the reconquest in 1692. After de Vargas had taken Santa Fé, he set out against some more distant villages. "The Indians of the Taos pueblo, who dwelt in a beautiful and fertile valley some seventy-five miles to the North, continued to be very hostile toward their brethren who were disposed to acknowledge the authority of the Spaniards, and Vargas had been requested by the Tanos, Teguas, and some of the Picoris Indians, to exterminate them."[2] Arrived at the pueblo, he found it deserted. The Indians had fled to the mountains. They were, however, induced to return, and quiet was restored.

Again in 1694 de Vargas was compelled to march on Taos. As before he found the village deserted, and when the people refused to return to their homes, he sacked the town.

The last time when the Taos people gave any trouble was at the time of the Taos rebellion in 1847. The country was disturbed owing to the relations between the United States and Mexico, and the insurrection was brought about more by the Mexicans than by the Indians themselves. The ruins of the church within which the Pueblo

[1] *Papers Arch. Inst. of Amer.*, III, p. 139, footnote.
[2] Davis, *The Spanish Conquest of New Mexico*, p. 341.

people made their last stand against the white people are still at Taos. The Pueblo Indian has always shown himself brave and ready to fight when occasion required, but peaceable and friendly toward those with whom cordial relations existed.

The final word has yet to be said on the linguistic relations of the Pueblos of New Mexico. Five groups may be recognized—Tiguas, Tehuas, Queres, Jemez, and Zuñi. Mr. Powell in his "Indian Linguistic Families North of Mexico"[1] includes Tiguas, Tehuas, and Jemez with the Tanos and Piros, the two latter of whom are extinct as distinct tribes, as Tañoan, thus giving but three stock languages among the New Mexican Pueblos.

The Tehuas occupy a compact group of villages in the Rio Grande valley — San Juan, Santa Clara, San Ildefonso, Nambé, Pojuaque, and Tesuque. The language spoken at these villages is not merely a series of dialects of one language, but is one and the same language, understood by all the people of all the villages. Before the Tanos became extinct as a tribe they lived about thirty miles south of the Tehuas,[2] and were the southern division of the same linguistic group. The Queres villages, Cochiti, San Felipe, Santo Domingo, Sia, Santa Ana, Laguna, and Acoma, while more scattered than those of the Tehuas, are not separated from one another by villages of another stock language. The Jemez and Zuñi occupy today but a single pueblo each.

In distinction from these present relations, the position of the Tiguas is peculiar; there is a northern and a southern group. In the north is Taos; about fifteen miles south from it across the mountains lies Picuris. These two villages are the homes of the northern Tiguas. Nearly ninety miles southwest in a direct line is Sandia, and twenty-five miles further south, Isleta, the two villages where the southern Tiguas now live. Between these two groups are all the pueblos of the Tehuas and certain of the Queres. Another noticeable thing about the Tigua pueblos is that the languages are not identical as are those of the Tehua towns, but differ so much that the people do not recognize them as being related to one another. An intelligent Taos Indian said to me: "When people tell you Picuris speak the same language we do, that is not true." He, however, admitted the Picuris people could understand them, although the Picuris language is not intelligible to the Taos people. Of the Isleta language he said he could

[1] Seventh Annual Report, Bureau of Ethnology.
[2] Papers Arch. Inst. of Amer., III, p. 125.

sometimes understand a word or two, and he thought the language would be easy for him to learn. In all probability practically the same statements might be made with reference to Sandia. They indicate simply that the separation of these four towns has been so long and so complete as to allow the languages to diverge from each other greatly, and this, too, in spite of the fact that Taos and Picuris are not more than fifteen or twenty miles apart, while only twenty-five miles separate Sandia and Isleta. It is true that the relations of towns, even of those belonging to the same linguistic stock, have not always been friendly, though their manners and customs have continued similar.

Mr. Powell includes the Moqui Pueblo languages, excepting that of Hano, in the Shoshonean family.[1] The connection of the New Mexican Pueblo languages with any of the great linguistic families is by no means so certain. In speaking of the Tañoan family, Mr. Powell says: "Recent investigations of the dialect spoken at Taos and some of the other pueblos of this group show a considerable body of words having Shoshonean affinities, and it is by no means improbable that further research will result in proving the radical relationship of these languages to the Shoshonean family. The analysis of the language has not yet, however, proceeded far enough to warrant a decided opinion."[2] Even if this relationship with the Shoshonean be established, the Queres and the Zuñi would still stand alone. Of the relation between them Mr. Powell says the "conclusion that they were entirely distinct has been fully substantiated."[3] If no connection can be established for certain of these groups, then they are either remnants of languages once more extensive, or cases of limited independent development of language.

Language is one of the important guides to relationship. The Indian himself can often tell you with confidence whence he came. We should be glad if we could meet the same problem with the same confidence. "'To regard the Pueblos of today as anything else but a mongrel breed, physically speaking, would be a grave mistake."[4] They have intermarried so long with the Navajos and Apaches, and to some extent with the Utes and other roaming Indians, that they are no longer of pure stock. This intermarrying has probably been much

[1] Seventh Annual Report, Bureau of Ethnology, p. 110.
[2] Ibid., p. 122.   [3] Ibid., pp. 138-9.
[4] Papers Arch. Inst. of Amer., III, p. 262.

more common since the coming of the Spaniards than before, so the
Pueblo people of three hundred and fifty years ago were of purer stock
than those of today. As Mr. Cushing has shown [1] the Zuñi to have come in part from
the south and in part from the north, and to have united to form one
people, so it may well be of the other village peoples that they are not
of one origin, but of several. With considerable regularity and per-
sistency the traditions of the Pueblo Indians, as well as those of some
Mexican tribes, refer to the north as their original home. To this fact
we must attach some significance. Northwesterly from the Pueblo
region are the ruins of the cliff and cave dwellers. Mr. Cushing has
explained the underground position of the kivas at Zuñi as the result
of years of life in the caves and cliffs, where lack of room necessitated
the building of these sleeping places for men outside of and below the
floor of the cave proper.[2] If this explanation be correct, as it seems
to be, the argument must apply with equal force to other towns than
Zuñi. At Taos and at Picuris the kivas are mainly underground.
This fact argues as plainly as in the case of Zuñi that a part at least
of the people were at one time living in the caves and cliffs of the cañon
region northwest of their present homes. Not alone the physical type,
but also the language, and perhaps, too, the customs and traditions, of
the Pueblos have been to some extent modified by intermixture with
outside tribes. Traditions and customs, however, we should expect
to change least.

Reference will be made later more specifically to certain traditions
related by the Taos people concerning their early home, but I think
we may with safety hold to the idea that most of them came from the
cliff-dwelling region, and that, after living for a time in several places,
they settled in the valley where they now live some time previous to
the coming of the Spaniards.

The number of the Pueblo Indians at the time of their discovery
has been variously estimated. The largest estimate is that of Antonio de
Espejo, whose total figures for all the Pueblos would give about 250,000.
From this number the estimates run all the way down to 23,000.
Vetancurt gives the figures for the year 1660 at a little over 23,000.[3]

[1] "Outlines of Zuñi Creation Myths," Thirteenth Annual Report, Bureau of
Ethnology, p. 343.

[2] *Ibid.*, pp. 344–5.

[3] *Papers Arch. Inst. of Amer.*, III, p. 121, footnote 1.

Bandelier says: "The villages of that time (first half of the sixteenth century) were on an average much smaller than those of today inhabited by Pueblo Indians, but there was a greater number of them. The aggregate population of the pueblos in the sixteenth and seventeenth centuries did not exceed twenty-five thousand souls."[1] Mr. Cushing says: "At the time of the Spanish conquest the Pueblo Indians numbered, all told, more than 30,000. . . . . The total population of the modern towns is about 10,000."[2]

Figures given in a Census Bulletin of the Eleventh Census show that in 1864, when the first complete and reliable enumeration in modern times was made, the Pueblo people of New Mexico numbered 7,066; in 1890 there were 8,287.[3] These figures show an increase in 26 years of 17 per cent. If the population in 1890 be compared with the conservative estimate of 1660 (23,000), a loss of 64 per cent. is shown. This falling off is to be explained by hostilities between the pueblos, by raids of roving Indians, by epidemic diseases, and perhaps by indirect effects due to contact with the whites. United States Indian Agent John Ward in his report submitted in June, 1864, says: "The greater number of the Pueblos are evidently on the increase, or at least . . . . the year 1863 has proved very prolific. Notwithstanding this, however, from all that can be learned and from many years of almost daily intercourse with these people, I am fully convinced that in the aggregate the pueblo population of New Mexico is gradually but surely decreasing."[4] This may have been true when it was written, but does not seem to be the case in more recent times, if the census reports may be relied upon. It has, however, to be admitted that the Pueblo people are very suspicious of government agents and of any white man who is inquiring into their affairs; so they frequently give inaccurate and incomplete answers.

The population of Taos in 1864 the same bulletin gives as 361. In 1890 it was 401. This is an increase of 11 per cent. in 26 years. The distribution as regards sex, age, and occupation is shown as follows: males, 213; females, 188; under 6 years of age, 52; over 5 and to 18, inclusive, 114; over 18, 235; over 70, 11; heads of families, 96; owners

---

[1] *Papers Arch. Inst. of Amer.*, III, pp. 120–21.
Castañeda gives 71 pueblos. Today there are 26.
[2] *Johnson's Encyclopedia*, article "Pueblo Indians."
[3] "Eleventh Census of U. S., Extra Census Bulletin," *Moqui Pueblo Indians of Arizona and Pueblo Indians of New Mexico*, p. 90.
[4] *Ibid.*, p. 80.

of houses, 96 ; farmers, 114 ; herders, 4 ; day laborers, 33.[1] With regard to sex this is perhaps correct enough, but as many even of the young men do not know their own ages, the numbers by ages cannot be relied upon, nor is it likely that the other figures are more than approximately correct. However, they give an idea of the numbers of the children and the occupation of the people.

During the time I was at Taos, three months in the summer of 1896, two deaths occurred, both those of very young children, and a few months after I left I learned of the death of a woman of about 50 years of age. During that same period of three months there were no births. Of course no importance can be attached to observations extending over so short a time. As nearly as I could learn from Americans living at the county seat three miles from the pueblo, the village has been just about holding its own during the last six years.

Land tenure among the Pueblo Indians, as with other sedentary Indians, was tribal, for their social organization was tribal. Owner-ship of land was the ownership of a range by a tribe. This range had no well-defined limits. Between a given tribe and its nearest neighbor there was often a debatable ground to which neither had undisputed claim, but no definite line separated the two areas. The tribe fre-quently moved within its own area. This continued for many years after the Spaniards gained control of New Mexico. And the prevail-ing customs of land tenure were not interfered with by the order of the king of Spain, which, according to Mr. Bandelier, "laid the foundation of the so-called Pueblo Grants of New Mexico."[2] In another place it is stated : "The so-called Pueblo Grants are not grants, they are limitations placed to the erratic tendencies of the sedentary, or rather land-tilling aborigines. Previously the villages were moved about within the range at will, and upon the slightest provocation."[3] These orders were simply to say to the Indians that land outside the limits laid down did not belong to them, and was not to be used by them. It is practically these same grants which the Indians hold today.

Tribal ownership of land in its simplicity implies that an individ-ual merely has the use of a certain amount of land, and that, when he no longer uses it, it again becomes common property. But contact

[1] "Eleventh Census of U. S., Extra Census Bulletin," *Moqui Pueblo Indians of Arizona and Pueblo Indians of New Mexico*, p. 92

[2] *Papers Arch. Inst. of Amer.*, III, p. 202.　　　　[3] *Ibid.*, p. 155, footnote.

with other peoples is bringing changes in the custom of tribal ownership. It is true Mr. Bandelier, in speaking of the individual owner of
land, says: "If he fails to cultivate it, or to have it cultivated for the
space of a year, the tract reverts to the commonalty, and is at the dis-
posal of the next applicant for tillable soil." [1] I very much doubt if
this is still true at Taos. While I cannot speak positively about it, I
believe the Taos Indian may do what he pleases with his land, till it,
lease it, let it lie fallow, or sell it, so long as he does not sell it outside
the tribe.

The Pueblo of Taos today has a grant of twenty-seven and a half
square miles, or $17,360\frac{55}{100}$ acres, according to the records of the Indian
agency at Santa Fé, and it is so stated in a bulletin of the last census.
But Captain Bullis, the Indian agent, informed me that years ago, when
the pueblo was often in danger of attack from other Indians, Mexicans
had been allowed to settle on the grant on condition that they would
assist in defending Taos against its enemies. They occupied about
one-half of the grant, and, as ten years' undisputed possession of land
in New Mexico gives title, the Indians, in reality, have today but one-
half the number of acres mentioned. The pueblo itself lies close to
the mountains, and a considerable portion of this land is mountainous.
That which lies along the creeks is excellent pasture land, but there
remains a great deal which can never be of any use except for mining.
The uncultivated land is today, as the whole area undoubtedly was at
one time, owned in common by the pueblo. The pasture lands in the
foothills, and the mesa land north and west of the village, still lie
open for the use of anyone in the pueblo. The only valuable piece of
land which is not owned individually, and which is near the village, is a
common pasture of twenty or more acres. It is so poorly fenced that
everyone who has horses, cattle, or burros, must take his turn watching
the stock to prevent their wandering out into the fields of grain.

At Taos, as everywhere else, some men are more prosperous than
others; so the amounts of land owned vary greatly. The sections of
land are small, but one man often owns several pieces, separated from
one another by one or two miles. "The fields behind the town towards
the mountain are divided by scrub willow, wild plum, and blackberry
bushes, and seldom contain more than three or four acres." [2] A fence is

---

[1] *Papers Arch. Inst. of Amer.*, III, p. 272.

[2] "Eleventh Census of U. S., Extra Census Bulletin," *Moqui Pueblo Indians of
Arizona and Pueblo Indians of New Mexico*, p. 100.

not often seen. There is a fence the greater part of the distance around the common pasture, and there are, besides, a few pastures belonging to certain families which are fenced. Sometimes a rude, temporary fence is built along a roadway when growing crops are in the fields near by. The boundaries between the plots of ground are usually irrigation ditches, along which grow plum bushes and willows. These are often very dense, and furnish a satisfactory and effectively marked line.

Just east of the pueblo is a break in the mountain chain. Down this gap comes Pueblo creek, the principal stream upon which the people are dependent for their water. It would be hard to find in the most favored parts of New England a more attractive place than is this stream for several miles along its course above the pueblo. It is filled with trout, shaded by willows, choke cherry, and cottonwood trees, and bordered with underbrush. The trees end abruptly at the pueblo, and where the stream flows through the town both banks are clear except for a few low bushes. But just below the town the fringe of willows begins again and extends for half a mile or more. The people believe that if the trees above the town were cut down the water would dry up, so no one is allowed to cut them. Very likely there is some ground for this fear, though perhaps the Indians have not reached the real explanation. At one time, many years ago, there were trees growing along. the banks within the town itself. One day a boy was lying asleep down by the stream under the trees and was killed by marauding Indians, who, sheltered by the trees, had slipped into the heart of the town unobserved. This was probably but one of many similar attacks. Then, too, my friend somewhat naïvely explained to me, they had to clean up under the trees every spring. So they cut them down and cleared up the banks.

About two miles above the village the first irrigation ditches branch off from the creek. Three or four main ditches tap the stream on each side, and these ramify into small channels until the whole of the cultivated area is reached. There are other ditches to bring water from Lucerro creek, which comes down from the mountains a short distance north of Pueblo creek. One of the larger ditches was made by the Indians years ago, under the direction of the priests, to carry water to a mill about three miles away. It is still used, but now only for irrigation.

Every Indian pueblo had to solve the problem of defense. Some-

times the solution was found on a high mesa, as at Acoma, or in a hollow square arrangement of the buildings, as at Tesuque, or in a wide, open plain. The villages were often located near some high mountain, mesa, or cliff, to which the people could flee in time of danger. As the Zuñi fled to To-yo-a-la-na, the Taos people several times abandoned their homes and took refuge in the foothills beneath the great Taos peak, which they call Sul-hwa-tu-na.[1]

But at Taos there was no cliff on which to build ; there was no wide, open plain. The Indians might have built their village as a hollow square, but instead they built great, high houses and surrounded them by a wall. This wall is now not more than four feet high, but it still surrounds the original area of the village, and one may still see the loopholes which were left to shoot through at the enemy outside. The original height of the wall was about eight feet. A walled pueblo seems to have been unusual. Castañeda speaks of a wall surrounding Cicuyé, which has been identified with Pecos. " Le village est environné en outre d'une muraille de pierre assez basse."[2]

Of the high houses at Taos there are two, one on each side of the creek which flows through the center of the town. "Taos and Zuñi are the only pueblos with four and five storied buildings, and the former may be called the old-fashioned pueblo *par excellence*, with its two tall houses sheltering the entire tribe of four hundred souls."[3] At one time, without doubt, the two main houses did shelter the entire tribe, but today small groups of buildings, one or two stories high, have been built both within the old wall and outside. Today the people do not live in as small a space as they once did.

These great houses were once communal, were owned by the people in common. There are still memories of such a condition. Today a single one of the many rooms, or two, or even three or four, are owned by individuals, and pass down from father to son or daughter, but do not revert to the community.

The great houses are spoken of by some writers as six and seven, and even as nine, stories in height. However high they may have been once I do not know. Certain it is that today the North House is five stories high, and the South House but four stories. The height

---

[1] On a map issued with the reports of the " U. S. Geographical Survey West of 100th Meridian " the elevation of Taos peak is given as 13,447 feet.

[2] H. Ternaux-Compans, *Voyage de Cibola*, p. 177.

[3] *Papers Arch. Inst. of Amer.*, III, p. 265.

of the buildings could not be increased more than one story, if the stepped form were retained, except, of course, by enlarging the base of the pyramid, for the highest story of each of the houses has but two or three rooms. Mr. Lummis speaks of the houses as pyramids,[1] and so they appear, irregular, and receding by four or five great steps to the top. The ground floor covers a large area, according to Mr. Davis about three or four hundred feet by one hundred and fifty for each building.[2] The second story recedes by the depth of one room, the third story recedes again, and so on to the top story. Today, with few exceptions, entrance may be had to the rooms through doorways. Not long ago the lowest story at least had no doorways. Mr. Davis speaks as if the upper tiers of rooms as well were without doorways,[3] but it seems more likely that all the rooms, excepting those of the first story, always had openings in the side walls for the people to pass in and out, though the doors themselves were of Spanish introduction. Mr. Victor Mindeleff, in his *Study of Pueblo Architecture*, says : "In ancient times the larger doorways of the upper terraces were probably never closed, except by means of blankets or rabbit-skin robes hung over them in cold weather. Examples have been seen that seem to have been constructed with this object in view, for a slight pole, of the same kind as those used in the lintels, is built into the masonry of the jambs a few inches below the lintel proper."[4] Plainly, in his opinion, there were doorways in the upper stories even in ancient times.

The only entrance to rooms in the first story was through a trap-door in the roof. One had first to climb a ladder to the roof, and then climb down another ladder into the room below. The terraced form of the houses gave a landing in front of the rooms on every floor, from which the people climbed to the rooms above. The ladders are still in use and are convenient and simple enough. Even though the houses are not the same which the Spaniards saw, they probably present much the same appearance, except for the doors and the chimneys which the Indians have learned from the Spaniards to make. The chimneys are low and stumpy, built usually of adobe and often capped with a broken pot.

[1] *Land of Sunshine*, Vol. VI, p. 141.   [3] *Ibid.*, p. 343, footnote.

[2] Davis, *The Spanish Conquest of New Mexico*, p. 343. footnote.

[4] "A Study of Pueblo Architecture in Tusayan and Cibola," Eighth Annual Report, Bureau of Ethnology, p. 182.

The windows of the Taos houses have not changed much since ancient times. They are usually small holes, a foot square or less, left in the wall near the ceiling and intended only to admit light. In summer they are uncovered and in winter are often closed up altogether. I have never seen gypsum used for window panes, as it is at other pueblos. A curious instance of the conservatism of the people is seen in the fact that within the limits of the old wall the use of glass in the windows is not allowed. Outside this wall in a few more modern houses one sees a glass window or two.

The interior of a room at Taos is very simple. I recall one in which a man, his wife, and two children were living. It was a room about seventeen feet square and ten feet high. It was built but a few years ago, and is unusually high, even for a modern room, for some are so low that one can just stand upright; in some of the older rooms one is even compelled to stoop when standing. The entrance to this room is on the north side near the northwest corner. In the middle of the north side is the fireplace, where the family cooking is done. A little three-legged, iron frame, used to hold pots over the fire, stands in the fireplace. Near by, on the floor, are two wooden boxes, about a foot square and four inches high, open at the bottom, and used for stools. Against the walls on the east and south sides are rolled up mattresses and blankets, ready to be spread out at night on untanned oxhides, which lie upon the floor. In one corner is a small table; near it a row of four or five shelves, on which are a few American dishes, some pottery cooking vessels, a little coffee, oatmeal, corn, and a few other things. In the middle of the west side is the metate, which every house must have. It is a large stone about two and one-half feet long by one and one-half wide, and set at an angle of about thirty degrees with the floor. A box is built around it so that none of the grain will be scattered as it is being ground. The whole is neatly plastered about with adobe. Several slabs of stone for grinding lean against the wall. A gun and a bow and arrows hanging from a peg, a pair of deer antlers and some turkey wings on the wall, and a few blankets thrown over a pole suspended from the ceiling, complete the furnishings of this home. The metates are used to grind only a part of the grain. The process is too laborious. It is much easier to load the grain on a burro, take it to a Mexican mill, and pay a certain proportion of it to have it ground.

Outside the houses in the open court of the pueblo, and in the

spaces between the houses, are many conical ovens built of adobe, and
varying from three to six feet in diameter. The Mexicans of the territory use the same sort of ovens, and it appears as if the knowledge
of them came to the Indians from the Mexicans. The principal use
to which they are put today is to bake wheat bread, and wheat came
with the Mexicans. "No example of the dome-shaped oven of pre-
Columbian origin has been found among the pueblo ruins, although its
prototype probably existed in ancient times, possibly in the form of a
kiln for baking a fine quality of pottery formerly manufactured.
However, the cooking pit alone, developed to the point of the
pi-gummi oven of Tusayan, may have been the stem upon which the
foreign idea was engrafted." [1]

Behind each of the great houses, just outside the village proper,
are several immense heaps of ashes and rubbish, the accumulation of
many years.

The principal crops of Taos are corn and wheat. Occasionally a
field of oats is seen, or a few beans and peas and melons. Considerable
quantities of squashes are also raised. Much of the corn and wheat is
sold at the stores three miles from the pueblo or traded for meat,
sugar, coffee, syrup, soap, cloth, or whatever else the Indian wants or
can buy. What game he can get, deer, turkeys, grouse, rabbits, and
doves, supplements his other supplies, though much less than it once
did, when game was plenty and methods of cultivation were much
more crude than now.

In summer the work of the men is, of course, mainly farming. But
the Indian farmer is not a very hard worker. At certain times, in
harvest time for example, or when he is irrigating, he has to work hard
and steadily, but ordinarily he works a part of the day and sits on the
housetop or goes to town for the rest of the day. When spring
comes and planting time is at hand, the land has first to be irrigated.
Two or three days later it is ready for the plow. By the hour I have
watched the planting of corn. Save for the figure of the Indian himself one would not know but that it was an American farmer at the
plow. Indian ponies, less often oxen, are used. Behind the one
following the plow comes an old man or a boy dropping the kernels
of corn which the next turning of the furrow will cover. After the
field is planted, the oxen are hitched to a long pole by rawhide traces
fastened to the yoke and to each end of the pole. An Indian steps

[1] Eighth Annual Report, Bureau of Ethnology, p. 164. See illustrations.

on the pole and, holding on by the tails of the oxen, rides around the field to level it off. When the corn is a few inches above the ground, the field is trenched for irrigating. After this there is, of course, the hoeing, hilling, and occasional irrigating. If the water is scarce, as it is in July, one has to engage the use of it several days beforehand and has to use it whenever it is assigned to him, whether it be day or night. I have several times known an Indian to work in the field irrigating all night after having worked all day, and sometimes even two nights in succession.

Modern American plows are commonly used. I have, however, seen at Taos two old home-made plows. They consist simply of a long straight pole, another short pole fastened to it at the proper angle, well braced and shod with a small piece of iron. Such a plow, of course, merely breaks up the soil and leaves a small trench; it does not turn a furrow.

The harvesting of wheat is a most laborious task. It is done with a small sickle. A few stocks of grain are grasped in the left hand, cut off with the sickle, and laid on the ground; then a few more, and so on. Where the soil is poor and the wheat scattered and poorly headed, the crop would seem to us hardly to repay the labor expended. At San Ildefonso, where much of the soil is sandy, I saw the Indians patiently harvesting such grain. But at Taos the wheat is vigorous and well-headed, and yields a good crop. The threshing is an interesting sight. A circle of tall poles is set up. Then the ground within the circle and for a space outside is wet and packed hard by a flock of sheep or goats. As the Taos Indians do not keep sheep and goats, a Mexican is hired to come with a flock and drive them around till the plot is hard almost as baked clay. A fence is then built and the harvested grain heaped up within the inclosure. One or two men stand on top of the pile to pitch down the grain into the circle just outside, while others drive the sheep or the goats around and around till the grain is threshed. Sometimes horses are used, but sheep or goats are much preferred. It only remains then to remove the straw and sweep up the wheat and the chaff from the hard floor. The Mexicans thresh in the same way. It is from them undoubtedly that the Indian learned how to thresh wheat, as it is from them he learned how to cultivate it.

Besides farming the men have occasionally to build a new house or to repair an old one, to go to the mill with grain, or to do some communal work. A few of them hire out to Americans or Mexicans to work in the field, to build a house, or to do other work. The pleasantest work which the Indian has to do is to go hunting. It is true game is not abundant, but sometimes two men will get eight or nine deer in a ten-days' or two-weeks' trip. They find a double pleasure in the deer hunt. They enjoy being away in the mountains free and alone, perhaps because centuries past they led such a life much more than now. And then, of course, they get the skins and the venison. The skins they use to make leggings, moccasins, and sometimes shirts. In winter they have little to do except hunt and bring wood from the mountains. To get wood with the Indian means, not to cut down trees and split them up, but to pick up small dry pieces, such as can be easily broken to a length suitable to being made into a pack for a burro. This is the life of the male Indian -- farming, hunting, house-building, making skin clothing, bringing wood, and sitting around.

The work of the woman is mainly in the house. She cooks, keeps the house clean, does the washing, cares for the children, and makes her own dresses. She has also to take care of the wheat and maize after it has once been harvested. The wheat she winnows in the most primitive way. She then washes it all in the creek to get rid of the chaff which remains after winnowing. This is done by partially filling a coarse basket made of yucca blades with the wheat. The water is allowed to run in through the basket, and the light chaff rises to the surface and is carried away by the running water. The wheat is then spread out in the sun and allowed to dry, after which it is carefully picked over by hand to find the little pebbles and sticks which may still be left. When all this is done, it is ready to be put in sacks and loaded on a burro to be taken to the mill. Sometimes one sees a woman driving the burros to the mill, but the men usually go. The women do not work in the fields except occasionally hoeing the corn, and this seems to be because they enjoy it rather than because it is at all necessary. A few women, however, widows and unmarried women, carry on the lighter work of farming quite regularly. The care of children, except when they are very young, is not great. They are obedient and deferential to parents, grandparents, and even to uncles and aunts. The little girls, even when not more than seven or eight years old, take care of the younger children, while the parents are at work.

At Taos today there is no spinning or weaving done. Some pottery is made, but it is of poor quality and is made only by a few old women and poor families.[1] The best pottery they get from the Tehua pueblos in exchange for wheat. The people say they used to make fine decorated ware, having learned from the Zuñi.

One of the most curious, and at the same time most characteristic, features of an Indian pueblo is its kivas, or estufas, as they are more commonly called. At Taos they are circular structures, built almost wholly underground, and entered by a single opening in the roof. There is no other opening in the room, save a small hole at one side to secure a draft for the fire. These kivas have come to be used as places for holding the civil, religious, and secret ceremonies of the tribe, but they were originally the sleeping and lounging places of the men, and could not be entered by the women except to carry food to their husbands, sons, and brothers.[2]

At most of the ruined towns and at most of the existing pueblos, the kivas were nearly or entirely underground, and they are usually circular. Eight ruined towns mentioned by General Simpson all had circular kivas, the number at the different towns varying from one to seven.[3] At Santa Clara today one, at least, of the kivas is above ground and is square. I do not know how many others there may be nor what their form and position are. At Picuris and at Nambé they may also be seen above ground, but round. So there is now considerable variation. There is, of course, variation in size, too, but they are usually high enough so that one can stand erect, and about twenty feet in diameter.

For the subterranean position of these rooms Mr. Cushing has offered the following explanation:[4] when the ancestors of these people were living in the caves and cliffs, the women built the houses and used them for the protection of themselves and their children. As

<hr/>

[1] Mr. Stevenson says : "The Pueblo tribes of New Mexico and Arizona, with rare exceptions, manufacture earthenware vessels for domestic use. The Pueblo of Taos may be mentioned as one of these exceptions." (Illustrated catalogue of the collections obtained from the Indians of New Mexico and Arizona in 1879. Second Annual Report, Bureau of Ethnology, p. 327.) This certainly is not true today.

[2] *Papers Arch. Inst. of Amer.*, III, p. 143 ; *Voyage de Cibola*, p. 170.

[3] "Journal of a Military Reconnaissance from Santa Fé, N. M., to the Navajo Country," Sen. Exec. Doc. 64, 31st Cong., 1850, 1st Session, Vol. XIV, pp. 55 *et seq.*

[4] "Outlines of Zuñi Creation Myths," Thirteenth Annual Report, Bureau of Ethnology, pp. 344 *et seq.*

KIVA AT TAOS WITH PALISADE AROUND ENTRANCE

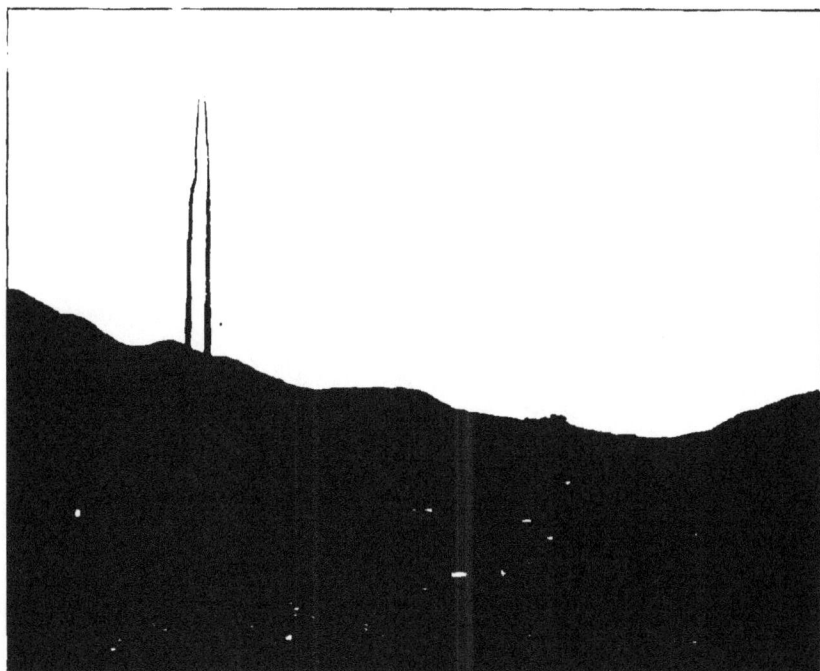

KIVAS AT TAOS WITH SQUARE WALL AROUND ENTRANCES

the level space was small, the men built sleeping and lounging places for themselves in the outer part of the cave, where the floor began to slope to the valley below. The walls were built only high enough to bring the roof up to a level with the cave floor. Thus the double purpose was accomplished of providing a common room for the men and of increasing the floor space in the caves. When the people left their cliff houses and came to live in the valleys, they continued to build their houses and kivas in the same old way, though the necessity for so doing had passed. The semicircular form of the villages to be seen in several of the ruined towns has not persisted in any of the existing pueblos, but the kivas are still usually subterranean or partially so. At the time of the coming of the Spaniards the youths and men slept in the kivas and spent only a part of the day time with their mothers, wives, and children. The Spaniards taught them to live in families, and one of the uses of the kivas was gone. They continue to be used on occasions of dances and for council meetings of the chiefs and other important gatherings of the men. Yet I have night after night seen the governor at Taos meeting his council in a room which he himself owned, and set apart for the purpose during the year he was governor. It may be that this is done because it is more convenient, or it may be that the governor and his council, since they have resulted from Spanish influence, are of less dignity and so meet in a less ceremonious way.

Another interesting thing about the kivas is their location. In the ruined pueblos, and to some extent in the modern ones, they are located outside the main mass of rooms, or at least outside of what constituted the original village. In many of the present towns they are found also in the open courts, or even within the great houses themselves. Of course, it may be that in these cases, too, the village has grown around the kivas, which were once on the edge of the town.

At Taos there are seven kivas, four on the south side of the creek, and three on the north side. Three of those on the south side are outside the old town wall and a few rods away from it. The other one and the three on the north side are within the wall. Bandelier says of the kivas at Taos that they are "completely subterraneous."[1] This is not today strictly true. The side walls of several of them can be seen for about a foot from the top. It may be that they were once entirely subterraneous and that the earth has worn away from them, though,

[1] *Papers Arch. Inst. of Amer.*, III, p. 268.

from the height of the roofs and from the general level of the ground around, I am led to think the earth had been banked up around them to give them the appearance of being wholly underground. This holds true more particularly of the kivas within the town wall.

It has occurred to me that these kivas in the old area of the town may be older than the three outside. There are two points which suggest this. In the first place, one would not expect that the sleeping rooms for men and youths would be built outside the inclosing wall and so unnecessarily exposed to danger of attack. It seems much more likely that they would be located near the edge of the town, in the most dangerous place, but not needlessly exposed. This is the position of the four kivas within the inclosing wall. In the second place, the construction of the kivas inside the wall differs in one particular, at least, from that of those outside. The roofs of all of them are flat, with the opening in the center. But those within the old town limits have this opening surrounded by a circular palisade of wood about seven or eight feet high. There is a narrow gap permitting one to pass inside the palisade. The kivas outside the town wall have the opening surrounded by a wall of adobe, a narrow gap being left as in the case of the others. This wall is only about two feet high, and the space inclosed, though of about the same size as that inclosed by the palisades, is square. I inquired as to the reason for this difference of construction, but was unable to find out anything about it.

I have been in but one of the kivas at Taos. One descends by a ladder, the two poles of which extend high up into the air. The room is just high enough for one to stand erect, and the ceiling is covered with soot from the fire which is lighted in the fire-pit in the center of the room on the occasion of any ceremony. One or two untanned ox hides lie on the floor, and a big drum, the skin of which is buffalo hide. I think the other kivas do not differ essentially from this one, save in the external details already mentioned.

An interesting illustration of the old-time use of the kivas for men and youths only came to my notice. A party of Taos men went with a small company of Utes to Indian Territory. On the return, when within a ride of a day or two of the pueblo, two men were sent ahead to notify the people of their coming. But instead of coming into the town they told the first person whom they saw to tell the war captain that they had come, and went themselves into a kiva. The war captain then notified the men of the village, and as many of them as wanted to went to the kiva where the messengers were. The messengers were given cigarettes to smoke and told to tell only the truth. They then told the story of the trip from the time of leaving the pueblo till they came back. But the women could not come to hear the account, but must hear about it afterwards. This, the people say, is an old custom, and so it undoubtedly is. It seems as if the explanation might be found in this : many years ago, when the kivas were the sleeping places of the men, it was natural enough that the men should go there on their return from a trip. Now, though the conditions have changed, the old custom is kept up.

Of the number of kivas in a pueblo Mr. Bandelier says : "It is probable that, as in Mexico, there were in each pueblo as many estufas as there were clans."[1] This may have been the case. It will not be easy to learn definitely, as some of the clans have disappeared, and certain of the kivas may have fallen to ruins and all trace of them been lost. The number of kivas at Taos at present does not agree with the number of clans which Bandelier says existed there. He says there were thirteen gentes, and gives the names of six. If these kivas were built at different times, and if there is any connection between the number of kivas and the number of clans, we seem to have evidence of an increase at some time in the number of the Taos gentes. This might easily be from division of gentes. It may be, too, that somewhere within the great houses are other kivas which the outsider knows nothing of.

Speaking of Taos, Mr. Poore says, in one of the census bulletins : "This is the most independent of the Pueblo tribes both in material condition and in its attitude toward strangers."[2] This freedom from outside influence is seen in the dress of the people. In many of the pueblos one frequently sees men wearing old trousers, vests, and hats, and American shoes. At Taos you may see one or two men wearing shoes, but you will not see old American clothes worn. Their clothes are made usually of American cloth, but, excepting the shirts worn by the men, are made in their own style.

The dress of the men consists of a common, American-made, colored shirt, cotton or woolen, according to the time of year ; a pair of leggings made of cheap worsted goods, or of blue or white drilling or

[1] *Papers Arch. Inst. of Amer.*, III., p. 144.

[2] "Eleventh Census of U. S., Extra Census Bulletin," *Moqui Pueblo Indians of Arizona and Pueblo Indians of New Mexico*, p. 100.

duck. Each of these leggings is made of a single piece of cloth, sewed together so that it will fit close to the leg and leave the edges of the cloth free to a length varying from one inch to six inches, or even more. The leggings come about half way up the thigh and are held up by a string which is attached to a cord passing around the waist. This same cord also supports the breech-clout, or G-string, as it is more commonly called in New Mexico. This is simple a strip of cotton cloth about six inches wide and varying in length. Sometimes it is long enough to touch the ground, both in front and behind. The moccasins, which are the common Indian moccasins, usually undecorated except with diamond dyes, are made either of buckskin or of leather taken from an old pair of American boots. The blanket which is worn about the loins or carried thrown over the shoulder is of American make usually. Occasionally leggings of buckskin are worn, and still more rarely a buckskin shirt. They are valued highly and are very durable, but since deer have become so scarce are not at all common. A hat is almost never worn by a Taos Indian. My friend, when we were going off for a week together, would give me his hat to carry till we were some distance away from the village, and then he would put it on. I suppose he wished to avoid the criticisms of the other men.

The man's dress is inexpensive, simple, and comfortable. That of the woman is equally so. At Taos women's dresses are made entirely of American goods. The one garment which has sleeves is a loose undergarment of white cotton cloth or some light print made like a night gown. It is plain, except for a little ruffle about the neck and wrists. Of these garments the women often have but one, so that, when it has to be washed, she must go partly dressed. If it happens to be stolen, as was that of one woman whom I knew, she must go without till she can make another. Their other dresses, of which they have many, are very simple, and are made of light and dark prints. Two strips of cloth, long enough to make the dress large enough around, are sewed together. The ends of this wide piece, except about one quarter of its length at the top, is then sewed together. About three inches of the upper end, near the open side, are sewed together, and the dress is done, except sometimes for a small worsted tassel at the lower end of the side seam. The little place at the upper end which is sewed together rests upon the right shoulder and holds up the upper part of the dress. The right arm passes through on one side of this little seam and the head and left shoulder on the other. This, of course, leaves the right arm and left shoulder and arm uncovered, except by the under-garment. Several of these outer garments are worn at the same time. All the women's dresses are of such a length that, if worn loose, they would nearly reach the ground, but they are held up about the waist by a belt so that they come just below the knees. The making of these belts is a native Indian industry, though they are now made at only a few pueblos. At Tesuque there are one or two men who still make them, but most of them seem to come from Jemez and other pueblos farther west. The weaving is close and firm, and the belts are very durable. The patterns of many of them are very pretty, red, green, and dark blue colors predominating.

The moccasins of the women are made of buckskin, sometimes of goatskin, and are long enough to come up just below the knee, where they are tied about the leg. The sole is of rawhide like those of the men's moccasins. A wash of white earth, easily renewed when necessary, is rubbed over the buckskin. The making of the moccasins is a part of the work of the husbands and fathers, who take pride in having their wives and daughters provided with strong, well-made pairs. These moccasins give to the women a very neat and rather picturesque appearance. The little girls wear the same sort of moccasins, but their dresses are more simple. When outdoors the women usually wear a shawl over the head. This is of American manufacture.

On dance days and other festival occasions the women wear much finer dresses than those mentioned above. These holiday dresses are of silk and velvet, and in place of a shawl a sort of cape of silk is worn hanging from the shoulders. Many have a "best pair" of moccasins, too. They are of buckskin, but are made differently from those worn every day, consisting of two pieces to each moccasin. One is a very low moccasin coming up just above the ankle; the other piece is a long strip of buckskin which is wound about the leg up to the knee. They look much firmer and smoother than the ordinary moccasins. One or two silver rings, a bracelet or two, and a pair of earrings will make up the woman's attire.

Before the introduction of American cloths the women used to dress partly in skins and partly in cloth brought from the Moqui towns and traded to the Taos people. These Moqui cloths are still made and may be seen at some of the pueblos in the Rio Grande valley, though they are no longer in use at Taos.

The women bang their hair and let it fall down over their eyes or push it a little to one side. Behind, when hastily done up, it is in a double T-shaped knot, bound with a mass of bright-colored woolen yarn. When more care is given to it, it is arranged in two double T-shaped knots, one on either side of the head just behind the ears, and tied with yarn. A pad made of combings of their own hair is used as a body for the knots when two are made. The men braid their hair in two braids and let it hang on either side of the head in front of the shoulders. Yarn, often bright-colored, is braided in and tied at the ends.

I was not able to be at Taos on the great annual holiday, the day of the patron saint, San Geronimo, the 30th of September. It was so often referred to, however, that I learned something about it. One of the great features of the day is the foot race. It is a relay race, the runners starting at opposite ends of the course and each coming back to the starting point, when another runner on each side starts at once. The race is kept up until a runner on one side has overtaken one on the other, one side having thus covered the length of the race course more than the other.

One can readily see that if the sides are evenly matched the race is likely to be a long, exhausting one, especially when run under the hot New Mexican sun.

Only a breech-clout and one or two ornamental pieces of fur or cloth are worn. The body is, however, rubbed with a wash of white clay, which gives it a peculiar mottled appearance.

This race is run at Picuris just as it is at Taos, and it was at the former pueblo that I saw it. There the grown men were so few that some of the runners on each side were mere boys. After running for several times they came in to the goal so nearly exhausted as to be hardly able to run at all.

Not merely on San Geronimo day, but on every saint's day, there is a dance. Today the people do not enjoy this dancing as they once did. Some men, when ordered by the war captain to dance, send their wives instead, and thus escape the punishment which would otherwise follow their failure to appear. The dances have been somewhat affected superficially by Christian influence, but it is probable that within the kivas, particularly in winter, the people dance in the old-time way, even though the faith of many in the importance of it all be somewhat shaken.

As in all the other pueblos, so at Taos, the civil organization has undergone some changes during the last three hundred years. Of course, it is bound up with the esoteric and religious life of the people. An important and curious position is that of cacique, an officer whose duties have to do for the part most with secret and religious ceremonials. John Ward says, in speaking of the pueblos of New Mexico: "The cacique evidently has more to do with the administration of ancient rites than with any other business. The high regard, mingled with respect and affection, which is invariably shown him places him more in the position of an elder than any other we think of."[1] I am inclined to think the influence of the cacique has quite noticeably diminished during the last few years. This certainly seems to be the case at Taos. The present cacique is a middle-aged man, who secured the office, partly through the influence of Americans in the vicinity, at the death of the former cacique a few years ago. There was another man whom many of the people favored, and this disaffected party now say of the cacique that they "do not care for him." They have, too, no very kind words for those who were influential in giving him his office. The office is for life, but does not seem to be hereditary. Bandelier says: "The caciqueship may be — I am not yet positive — hereditary in a certain gens; but if this is the case, I hold it to be so only among the Tehuas, and not among the Queres."[2] From the fact that there were at Taos two parties representing candidates for the caciqueship one may infer that today at least there is no strict rule of inheritance of the office, though, of course, it may be that among the Tiguas, to whom the Taos people belong, it was hereditary in a gens, as is suggested it was among the Tehuas. From actual investigation I am unable to say what the duties of the cacique are, except the small part which he plays in the election of governor and war captain; this will be mentioned later. The impression prevails among the white people of the vicinity that the cacique is the keeper of the traditional, mythical, and sacred lore of the tribe. In fact, it was because it was thought the present officer would be more communicative in these matters that he was supported for the position by the Americans.

Mr. Bandelier further says,[3] in speaking of the Queres, that in former times, and often today, a piece of land was tilled by the com-

---

[1] "Eleventh Census of the U. S., Extra Census Bulletin," *Moqui Pueblo Indians of Arizona and Pueblo Indians of New Mexico*, p. 81.

[2] *Papers Arch. Inst. of Amer.*, III, p. 280.   [3] *Ibid.*, III, p. 281.

munity for the cacique. Besides he was exempt from communal work. While I am not certain, I very much doubt if this is now true at Taos, whether it may once have been or not. One fact which I learned points to the conclusion that at one time a certain amount of communal work was done for the cacique and suggests what his former position may have been. At the top of the great house on the south side was a room or two which belonged to an old woman. They fell to ruins and were rebuilt by the community and given to the cacique to occupy. It is there he is living today, but the rooms in all probability remain the property of the community.[1]

The part of the government of the pueblo with which an outsider first comes into contact is the governor. He is elected annually and takes office on the first day of January. Although the Indians maintain that this was the custom before the coming of the Spaniards, there can be no doubt that it is a change brought about by Spanish influence. The governor is elected by the chiefs and is the executive officer of the village. His business is to settle quarrels which arise between members of the tribe themselves, or between members of the tribe and outsiders, to see that the irrigating ditches are kept in repair, and to assign times to the men for the use of the water in irrigating. As the Mexicans have the use of the water of the creek three days in the week, they may often be seen at the governor's house talking with him about some misunderstanding which has arisen.

The governor, with nine officers who are chosen to assist him, has frequent meetings, often many nights in succession, to talk over matters. When any announcement is to be made to the people, he steps out on the roof of his own house, or climbs to some high place on one of the great houses, and gives his message in a voice loud enough to be heard over the greater part of the village. It is this custom which has led some to speak of the "town-crier,"[2] and there is some reason for the comparison. Sometimes the announcement is that they must send their children to school; again, that they must come out in the morning and plant the corn in the priest's field, or, that they must not turn

[1] On cacique see further, *Papers Arch. Inst. of Amer.*, III, pp. 276–84.

[2] "U. S. Geographical Survey West of 100th Meridian," VII, *Archæology*, p. 483: "The town-crier goes out every morning at seven o'clock to chant this strain of words, repeating it frequently, and another song is sung by him in the evening to close the day's work." It is doubtful if these announcements which are so frequently made, are in many cases to summon the people to work or to announce the close of the day's labor.

READY FOR THE RELAY RACE, SAN GERONIMO DAY, TAOS

GROUP OF TAOS INDIANS

all the water from the creek into the irrigation ditches above the pueblo, as the women are then obliged to go too far for water for household uses.

A man may be governor for several years. One old chief, who seems to be held in high esteem, and is one of the principal chiefs of the village, has been governor six or seven years, not, however, continuously. By virtue of having once held the office a man becomes a chief, at first one of the lesser chiefs, but he has a voice in the election of the succeeding governors.

The war captain, whose office seems to be second in importance to that of the governor, is also elected by the chiefs. He has a lieutenant and nine officers, making a board of twelve in all. He has charge of the dances which occur on festival days, and, assisted by his officers, gives orders as to who shall dance ; if his orders are not obeyed, the offender is arrested by the one of the officers whose special duty it is, and given a public whipping. The war captain also has charge of the communal meadow, and appoints each week those who are to watch the stock there and keep them from getting into the grain fields. Only those who have stock, cattle, horses, or burros, in the meadow are appointed to this duty. If some animal does get out into a cultivated field, it is the war captain's duty to find out whose it is, and to settle the fine to be paid by its owner to the owner of the field. Further, he has to do with trips which are sometimes made to some distant place, such as the trip to Indian Territory, mentioned above. He decides whether the people shall go, and it is to him they report on their return. His title, war captain, suggests what his duties may have been at one time. In all probability in his hands lay the defense of the town, but as there is no longer any occasion for defense, his office appears to be of less importance than it once was.

In holding these various offices certain rules are observed. When one is an officer of the war captain for the first time, he is the lowest officer ; the second time he is next to the lowest, and so on. After being an officer of the war captain one must wait one year before he can be an officer of the governor.

The important men of the town are the chiefs, their influence being much greater than that of the governor, unless, of course, the governor himself happens to be one of the principal chiefs. The importance of the chief appears to depend in part on the number of times he has been governor. Three chiefs, whose influence is greater than that of the others, play an important part in the election of the village officers. Two men are proposed by them for governor, and the other chiefs vote for the one of the two whom they prefer. The cacique counts the votes. If this really be the only part which the cacique plays in the election, it is insignificant enough. Bandelier says that among the Queres he chooses both the governor and the war captain,[1] and I suspect that the fact that my informant at Taos belonged to the party which was opposed to the present cacique led him to minimize his importance as much as possible.

After the selection of the governor, the war captain is chosen in the same way. The war captain's lieutenant is chosen from two of his officers, designated by the three chiefs. The other officers, those of the governor and of the war captain, are chosen by all the chiefs together. Besides these duties, the chiefs have in their hands the most important business of the tribe. Any trouble concerning the land which sometimes arises with the Mexicans, or any business connected with the United States government, that is, "big business," has to be dealt with by the council of chiefs. This statement concerning the officers and the chiefs was given to me by the son of one of the three principal chiefs.

Of the clans at Taos I was able to learn scarcely anything. I inquired several times of my friend there, but he always answered that he did not know about any such thing. Later he told me that he had asked his father, and his father had said to him: "You are around with the chiefs all the time and would hear about such things if we had them." I do not know whether he was absolutely ignorant of the gens or was simply unwilling to tell. He did, however, say that many years ago the Taos people numbered about 1,000. Part of them were living about one-eighth of a mile from the present pueblo, and were known as ha-chĭ-tĭ-pipl, or stone-axe people. They did not enjoy farming and so left the remainder of the people where they now are, and themselves journeyed away to the east. Two or three generations ago, when a party of Taos men were on a hunting trip 250 miles to the east, they came across some people who talked their language. They did not see the place where these people lived. It may be that these were the stone-axe people. Those now living at Taos call themselves ˌ-Tá-i-na-ma, or willow people. This term appears to apply to all those in the pueblo, and not to any one division of them. Of

---

[1] *Papers Arch. Inst. of Amer.*, III, pp. 283 and 285.

course, it may be that one clan has absorbed the others, or that all but one have died out or wandered away, so that but one of the original number remains today. But it seems far more likely that the people are exceedingly jealous in regard to this matter, and will not speak of it to an outsider till he has fully gained their confidence.

Bandelier says[1] there were thirteen gentes at Taos; of these he names the following six: the bead, water, axe, feather, sun, and knife clans, but he plainly says that he cannot guarantee the accuracy of the lists, so we should regard them as subject to correction.[2]

Neither was I able to learn whether marriage must be outside the clan still. If the clans really have become reduced to one, there could, of course, be no marrying outside the clan. The parents of a young man appear to have a good deal to say as to whom he shall marry, and, although some do marry against their father's and mother's wishes, it is not a common thing. One young man whom I knew was about to marry a girl of his own choosing, when he was induced by his parents to marry another. It was easy to see in talking with him that it was simply a matter of parental preference. He preferred one and his parents the other, and he yielded. While he does not today appear actually to regret his action, he does think often of his own choice in the matter.

An interesting survival, apparently of the time when a man went to live at the home of the woman whom he married, is to be found in one of the Taos marriage customs. After marriage the man goes to live with his wife at her home with her parents. The length of this stay depends upon circumstances. Then the young man and his wife build a new house or go to live in one which he already has.

The old method of reckoning time is interesting. It is not a method which would have been equally accurate and convenient at all of the New Mexican Pueblos because of their location. But as one looks west from the pueblo at Taos, the outline of the mountains is much broken; the varied forms of the hills have suggested names such as "pottery hill," "wolf's ear hill," "eyebrow hill," etc. Of course, between the winter and the summer solstices the sun appears to have

---

[1] *Papers Arch. Inst. of Amer.*, III, p. 273.

[2] I hope some day to make a complete census of the Pueblo of Taos, as has been done recently by Professor Starr for the Pueblo of Cochiti, including the Indian and the Spanish name, and the clan of every individual. "A Study of a Census of the Pueblo of Cochiti, New Mexico," Proc. Dav. Acad. Nat. Sci., Vol. VII, pp. 33-44.

moved every day a little farther north as it sets behind the hills. Between the summer and winter solstices the sun seems to be retreating toward the south. The Indians had noticed the exact place in the horizon where the sun set every day in the year, and they knew at just what time the sun would reach a certain point. They thus had the year exact—from the time when the sun reached its most southerly point on the horizon to the time when it returned to it again. They watched the sun set from a certain tree in the pueblo, because they had noticed that the place of setting was different according to the place from which it was observed.

They recognized four seasons : summer, called in the native idiom "good time;" autumn, "ripe time;" winter, "still time;" spring, "beginning time." This last refers, not to the growing grain and the budding trees and bushes, but to the work of the people themselves. The summer months are May, June, and July; the autumn, August, September, and October; the winter, November, December, January, and February; the spring, March and April. When one compares the names given to the seasons with the months which correspond to them, it is, I think, easy to see the reason for the differences between the Indian seasons and our own. One should remember also that Taos is high up in the mountains and hence probably has a long winter.

Undoubtedly in the old days the people did much more communal work than now. Individualism was not developed to any marked degree; the communal idea was the most prominent one. The houses and lands were common property, and, although a man had a few things which he himself owned, almost everything belonged to the tribe or to the clan. Although communal ownership and communal activity has now almost wholly passed away, one may still see lingering traces of it, as in the common meadow and in communal work. I have mentioned the work done for the priest. The priest baptizes and marries the people and helps them die, and in return they cultivate a field which is set apart for him. Wheat or corn, as he may wish, is planted, irrigated, and harvested for him. This work is done by all the men, called out by the governor as occasion requires. Wood is also furnished the priest. Every man brings a little to the governor's house, and this is then loaded on burros and taken to the priest's house at the American town of Taos.

Nothing remains of the old communal hunts, save an occasional rabbit hunt. These occur on the days before saints' days, when, of course, there will be a dance. A considerable number of the men and older youths ride away to the mesa six or eight miles, armed with bows and arrows, and sometimes with clubs. They drive the rabbits until they have rounded them up in a small area, and then kill them with arrows or with clubs. The rabbits are, I believe, cooked and given to the dancers the next day in the kivas.

The irrigation ditches have to be repaired occasionally and, as they are of use to all and belong to no one in particular, work on them is done by all in common.

One of the best illustrations of Indian conservatism I have seen was in connection with the old wall at Taos. The wall is now of no use, and has weathered down so that it is very low; yet, if a section of it happens to fall or to be knocked over, after a time it will be repaired. One day some of the men make the adobes ; a few days later others come out and, assisted by the women who carry the mud for mortar, rebuild the wall to its present average height. The only explanation given me was that it is an old custom, and doubtless this is the main, if not the only, reason for doing the work. There used to be a wall about the pueblo, therefore there must still be one.

One form of punishment at Taos is to compel the offender to do a certain amount of communal work. This is often the punishment for a man who does not appear in the dance, when he has been ordered by the war captain and his officers to do so. For offenders against tribal law there is a house used as a jail. This was in bad condition and has been lately repaired by the people. For a very serious offense, such as murder, a man is now sent to the territorial penitentiary at Santa Fé, but for lesser offenses the pueblo jail is used. One man I was told of who was kept in jail a week for refusing to live with his wife after he had been ordered to do so. She had been unfaithful to him, but after his week's confinement he consented to live with her again.

The linguistic relations of Taos I have already indicated. The language itself is rather soft and pretty, due in part to the many vowel sounds, particularly at the ends of the words. It is spoken so slowly and distinctly that one soon comes to understand a few of the words. But the people are exceedingly jealous of an outsider learning their language, and in order to gain a speaking knowledge of it, he would be obliged to live with the people, and completely gain their confidence.

My friend taught me a few words, but told me I was not to repeat them to anyone, or even to let anyone know I had learned them. Even these few words were taught me when we were alone, away from the pueblo, in the mountains.

The first afternoon I was at Taos a small boy of about eight years taught me the numerals up to twenty. He patiently repeated for me word after word, until I had them thoroughly learned. During the three months after that day I learned but one other word from him, and then only in confirmation of one which had been given me by another friend. He had, I suppose, been told by his parents that he must not teach the language to white people. At Taos, as at many other Indian pueblos, as among most Indians in fact, there is "a sort of sacred language." " Some linguists think that these dialects are archaic forms of the language, the memory of which was retained in ceremonial observances ; others maintain that they were simply affectations of expression and form a sort of slang, based on the everyday language, and current among the initiated."[1] Brinton is inclined to the latter opinion. Whatever be the source of this " sacred language," it is a very common thing. The Taos people, for example, have four or five different words for many things, but not more than one or two of these words are known to all the people. The others are known only to those who belong to some particular society, or who have been initiated into some special mysteries.

Every individual at Taos has two names ; first, his native Indian name, which is a single personal name, and does not indicate the family at all. Like other Indian names, they have definite meanings, and are often picturesque. A small boy whom I knew bore the name K'en-pi-oo-na — hare-track — because his father had noticed the track of a hare on the snow, and it was very straight and pretty. One girl was named Kwŏⁿ-fá-o — white, fleecy cloud — because such clouds are pretty. No two people have the same name, nor after the death of one is the name given again so long as it is remembered that the name has been used. Everyone has, also, a Spanish name, both a Christian name and a family name. It is by this name the Indian is known outside the village among whites and other Indians, though often it is not known to everyone in the village, since in the pueblo the native name alone is used.

Probably for hundreds of years men have occasionally gone from

[1] D. G. Brinton, *American Hero Myths*, p. 26.

their own native villages to live at others, where often their own, but sometimes another, language was spoken. The cause of this was, in many cases, some trouble at their own homes. From Isleta four men in recent times have come to live at Taos, have been received and allowed to adopt the customs of the people. They have married, and have had in the four families three children, who are as much children of the village as any others. A San Juan man, also, came and wished especially to watch the stock in the meadow ; he, too, was welcomed, married, and had two children. A very old Picuris man is living there, and has been there since he was a boy. There were two brothers at Picuris, both of whom were married, and one of whom had three children. They had trouble with some other men in the village, so one of them came up to Taos to ask the governor if they might come there to live. The governor consulted his council, and consent was given, so the brothers and their families came. This old Picuris man was one of the three children, and later married a Taos woman. These cases were told me by a friend at Taos, and simply illustrate the occasional movements of these people from their own villages to others, where the customs are more or less similar.

The social life of the Indian is so bound up with his esoteric and religious life that one cannot be fully considered without the other. But to speak of the religious life of the Indians, one must have lived with them so long as to fully gain their confidence. For this a few months are not sufficient. Mr. Cushing and Mr. Bandelier have shown in considerable detail to what extent the Indians are Catholics. The latter says : " The Pueblo Indians accepted the new faith voluntarily, and to a certain extent honestly. They adopted it, however, from their own peculiar standpoint, that is, they expected material benefits from a creed that pretended to give them spiritual advantages. In their conception, religion is but a rule of conduct controlling man while alive, and on strict compliance with which his success in this world depends. In short, the Pueblos looked upon Christianity as upon another kind of magic, superior to the one which they practiced themselves ; and they expected from the new creed greater protection from their enemies, more abundant crops, less wind, and more rain, than their own magic performances procured."[1] And again : " It is vain to deny that the southwestern village Indian is not (?) an idolater at heart, but it is equally preposterous to assume that he is not a sincere

[1] *Papers Arch. Inst. of Amer.*, III, p. 218.

Catholic. Only he assigns to each belief a certain field of action, and has minutely circumscribed each one." [1] I am not so much inclined to doubt that the village Indian is sincere as that he is a Catholic. If one may judge at all from the attendance at mass, he will certainly think that the hold of Catholicism at certain of the villages is weak. I have many times at Taos watched the few who answer the call of the little church bell on Sunday mornings. My friend said to me that they had another religion besides the Catholic, and that they did not care for the priest, and would not care if he should go away and not come back. This is nothing new, but it is important because the admission was made, for they always claim to be Catholics. Though the priest baptizes and marries the people, the native rites are added to the Catholic, otherwise the ceremony would not be complete.

There are some indications which lead one to think that the Pueblo Indian wants only the opportunity to take off his new religion like an outer garment, when beneath will appear the old, as it once was, worn at one or two points, to be sure, by these three hundred and fifty years of contact with the new creed, but still substantially the same. One may see at Taos an image of the Virgin Mary carried about the fields in the summer time to secure good crops. It is shaded by a rude awning, and accompanied by a few Mexican and Indian women, and some young men with rifles, which they occasionally fire off into the air. It is plain enough, I think, that practices like this indicate no adoption by the people of anything fundamental in the faith.

A little experience of my own rather curiously illustrates the Indian's attitude toward religious matters. Hanging in one of the houses at Taos was a small plate of hammered copper, on which was cut a design of " our lady of Zapopan." I wished to have it, as it seemed to have belonged to a printing press. At first it was promised to me, but when I finally asked to have it, it appeared that the woman to whom it really belonged had hidden it. She was afraid that if she parted with it, some harm might come to her two little children. Both she and her husband, who promised it to me, feared this, because they had known a man who met with an accident because he had sold a small image of a saint. After selling it, he had gone into town, bought some whisky, and then rode his horse home at a breakneck pace. The horse stumbled at a small bridge and broke his leg. This was, of course, *because* he had sold the little figure. Naturally, then,

[1] *Papers Arch. Inst. of Amer.*, III, p. 222.

they might expect some harm to befall their own family, particularly the helpless little ones, if they parted with the copper plate, and this, not so much because it had a design of the Virgin on it, which was sacred, as because of some power in it which would be offended.

On the whole, it seems to me that Mr. Cushing's view is the correct one, as he has outlined it in his study of "Zuñi Creation Myths." In one place he says : "The Zuñi faith, as revealed in this sketch of more than three hundred and fifty years of Spanish intercourse, is as a drop of oil in water, surrounded and touched at every point, yet in no place penetrated or changed inwardly by the flood of alien belief that descended upon it. . . . . He is slow to adopt from alien peoples any but material suggestions, these even, strictly according as they suit his ways of life ; and whatever he does adopt, or rather absorb and assimilate, from the culture and lore of another people, neither distorts nor obscures his native culture, neither discolors nor displaces his original lore." [1] Mrs. Stevenson, in writing of the Sia, says : "While the religion of the Rio Grande Indians bears evidence of contact with Catholicism, they are in fact as non-Catholic as before the Spanish conquest." [2]

It is not an easy thing to realize the face of tradition and custom. We rarely think how many things we do because it is customary, though the purpose which moved the makers of the custom is lacking with us. But the most conservative civilized people in the world can little appreciate the situation of men whose whole lives are dominated by one long series of traditions and customs, as are those of the Indians. They do many things simply because it is the custom, and can give no better reason for doing them. These conservative forces are growing slowly less in Indian life, as the people learn white men's ways and come under American influence. But as the Indian is only in the childhood of culture growth, he takes the forward steps but slowly, as all who have traveled the same road before him have done.

In the study of the traditional lore of the Pueblo people very little satisfactory work has been done. The mention of Mr. Cushing's name calls to mind the best illustration of such work. What he has done among the Zuñi should be done in every other pueblo, or, at least, in every one of the four or five related groups of people. His

---

[1] Thirteenth Annual Report, Bureau of Ethnology, p. 339.
[2] Eleventh Annual Report, Bureau of Ethnology, p. 14.

work, however, represents the labor of many years and of long residence at Zuñi.

In the traditions of the Pueblo people it is interesting to notice the resemblances which occur from one tribe to another, resemblances which are, as we should expect, closer between the Pueblos themselves than between them and outside peoples. The difficulty of learning anything from the Indians, particularly of a mythical or religious nature, is very great. It cannot be appreciated by one who has not made the attempt. So experienced an ethnologist as Mr. Bandelier says: "Notwithstanding a residence of over one year among the Queres, I never succeeded in penetrating their secrets more than partially."[1] If one once takes a false step, adopts a wrong method in dealing with them, his influence is gone. Bandelier speaks of Santo Domingo having closed its doors to him.

At Taos I was hampered in my inquiries by a circumstance which illustrates very well certain characteristics of the Indian. Some years ago, about fifteen I believe, representatives of the government were at Sia making investigations. Of course they had to ask many questions. Some time after they went away there was much sickness in the pueblo, and many people died. It occurred to the Sia people that the presence of those white men, asking a lot of questions, was the cause of all their trouble, so they sent men to the other pueblos to warn them against white men who came to find out about their customs and beliefs. These messengers were at Taos, and the people remember their warning well. If a Taos Indian is caught now teaching the language or telling any of the traditions to a white man, he is liable to a whipping and a fine. This accounts for the fact that I could rarely learn anything from my friend when we were at the pueblo, although when away in the mountains he became much more open and communicative.

The few myths which I was able to learn are brief, but they are outlines, and have some features which indicate connection with other pueblo myths.

The people of Taos came originally from the north, where they lived in what is now southern Colorado. After leaving this place they lived for some time in northern New Mexico, and again some miles east of their present home. But before living on the earth at all, they had lived *in* a lake. When they came up from the lake, they

---

[1] *Papers Arch. Inst. of Amer.*, III, p. 293.

were wild, did not wear even the breech clout, and began at once to hunt the deer. While in their northern home they had many neighbors, among them the Picuris, who lived just south of them. One day a Picuris man was planting some white corn. He had some grains in his hand and was showing them to a Taos man, when the latter hit his hand from below and scattered the corn. From that time the two peoples were enemies, and the Picuris moved away to the south. We note here agreement with other Pueblo myths in two points: first, that the people came from the north, and, second, that they had not always lived on the earth, and had not been created on it, but came up from below. The Zuñi myths, as given by Mr. Cushing, are very elaborate in their account of the way in which the people escaped from the lower world, the stages they reached, the guides they had, etc.[1] The Sia have a similar myth.[2] Among the Navajos there seems also to be the same idea,[3] though it very likely was borrowed from the Pueblo people.

Before the people came from the north, the earth was soft; even the rocks were not hard, so that animals left tracks in them, which can be seen in the hard rocks today. All the ground was covered with water. This is simply the widespread tradition of a flood, which has been explained as either local remembrance of actual floods, or as a conclusion arrived at from finding on high land shells of animals which live in water, or from the evidence furnished by these tracts in the rocks, which, to a primitive mind, must certainly be conclusive. A tradition of a flood may also have arisen from the teachings of missionaries. These sources are obvious enough. John Fiske says: "The numerous myths of an all-destroying deluge have doubtless arisen partly from reminiscences of actually occurring local inundations, and partly from the fact that the Scriptural account of a deluge has been carried all over the world by Catholic and Protestant missionaries."[4]

When the foremost of the men of the Zuñi first came forth, they found the earth "wet and unstable."[5] The men had webbed feet "like those of walkers in wet and soft places."[6] Later, after Zuñi-land

---

[1] Thirteenth Annual Report, Bureau of Ethnology, pp. 379-84.
[2] Eleventh Annual Report, Bureau of Ethnology, pp. 26-37.
[3] Eighth Annual Report, Bureau of Ethnology, p. 275.
[4] John Fiske, *Myths and Myth-Makers*, p. 152.
[5] Thirteenth Annual Report, Bureau of Ethnology, p. 381.   [6] *Ibid.*, p. 383.

had been settled, a flood came from the swelling of the river and buried houses and many men, and was stayed only when a youth priest and maiden priestess had been sacrificed to the waters.[1] The Sia also refer to a great flood which " did not fall as rain, but came in as rivers between the mesas, and continued flowing from all sides until the people and all animals fled to the mesa."[2] Here, too, to stay the waters a youth and maiden were cast " from the mesa top ; and immediately the waters began to recede."[3] To another feature of this tradition of a deluge at Taos reference will be made in connection with the Taos culture-hero.

The hero·was named Pi-an-kĕt-tă-chŏl-lă (Point hill green), a name which was given him because he could at any time, even in winter, make a hill green. This the people consider a very good name. Pi-an-kĕt-tă-chŏl-lă was born at the foot of a cedar tree about one hundred and fifty miles north of Taos and west of the San Luis valley. His mother, who was a Pueblo woman, had never known a man, but she put some very fine pretty pebbles in her belt, and soon after this child was born. When the people could not find out who the father of the child was, they attempted to put him to death. But they did not succeed, and as soon as he grew older he began to look very beautiful, "like Jesus Christ," one of the men said to me. Now there was a time when the Pueblo people did not know how to dance, to make their clothes, to plant corn, beans, and calabashes. After Pi-an-kĕt-tă-chŏl-lă came, he taught them all these things. He picked out some different-colored stones, and from them he made corn, beans, and calabashes grow.

He also had the power to fly. One time he went up to find out about the stars. He took off his moccasins and all his clothes except the breech-clout. Many people came out to see him. He had an eagle's tail fastened to his breech-clout behind, and on his arms above the elbow wild turkey wings. When there was too much wind, he could not go up ; but on a quiet day he would go to the top of a house and fly away. The people would watch him grow smaller and smaller, till finally he became small as a fly, and then disappeared altogether. He went up very high in the air, as high as from Taos to Santa Fé, and got within a few feet of the stars. They are birds and have very green legs and very bright breasts, like a humming bird ; they have a bill something like an eagle's, and very dark eyes. The twinkling of

[1] Thirteenth Annual Report, Bureau of Ethnology. p. 429.
[2] Eleventh Annual Report, Bureau of Ethnology, p. 35.   [3] Ibid., p. 57.

the stars is simply the birds flying slowly. The shooting stars are birds moving quickly from one place to another. When you cannot see the stars, the birds have turned around, so that their bright breasts can no longer be seen, and so they give no light. Pi-an-kĕt-tă-chŏl-lă could not find out how the birds live, nor could he get near enough to the sun and moon to find out about them.

But he could not only fly, he could also go down into the earth. In summer time he could bring up ice and snow, and in winter he could bring up green leaves. He could make rain come when he wished.

At one time there were many people living on the earth, but much hot water came and drowned them all. The whole earth, even the rocks, became soft. This wise man made a big pile of cottonwood bark and got inside the pile and so did not die. While the waters thus covered the earth, Pi-an-kĕt-tă-chŏl-lă looked down into the earth and saw it was all green there, so he made the water go down there. He then came out from the pile of bark and took some foam from the top of the water and made people. He took different-colored stones and made maize and other seed. These the people planted, and the next year the seed was distributed, and so they had crops again.

Before the Pueblo people saw white men, negroes, and all other people, this wise man had seen them and told the pueblo people about them. Of the Americans he had said that some time a people would come who made a noise with their shoes, like men walking on snow. The Indian who told me this added, with confidence : "This is true, because we see." He told them they would get fewer and fewer, and by and by would all be white men, and then there would be no more Pueblo people.

One cannot wonder that the influence and presence of white people is much disliked, especially when he considers that the birth of half-breeds is but a step toward the extinction of the Pueblo people, according to their own traditions.

Pi-an-kĕt-tă-chŏl-lă is still living in a lake somewhere to the north. One time a noise, like the beating of a drum, such as is now used in their dances, was heard *in* the lake. His tracks have been seen about there too. "He is very old, but does not die."

Po-shai-yān-ne, the culture-hero of the Sia, was born of a virgin at the Pueblo of Pecos. She became pregnant from eating two piñon nuts. At his birth she was much chagrined and cast him off, while he was still very young. He lived as best he could until he reached manhood, when his magic power appeared. After a time he went to visit all the pueblos. When he came to the Sia, they knew him, because they had heard of him. He stayed with them a while and taught them to hunt, and then went on into Chihuahua, Mexico. Here he was killed by rivals for the favor of a chief's daughter, to whom he had been married, but the next day he appeared alive again, and, though a second time put to death, by drowning, he rose again, and the Sia say : " He still lives, and some time he will come to us. . . . . He may come today, tomorrow, or perhaps not in our lifetime."[1]

Just as we find the Taos culture-hero Pi-an-két-tă-chól-lă making people from the foam on the water, so the Sun-father of the Zuñi impregnated the Foam-cap so that she gave birth to the Beloved Twain, who led men out from the world below to the world of light and life.[2]

The culture-hero of the Zuñi who corresponds most nearly, perhaps, to these of Taos and of Sia was Paí-ya-tu-ma, "God of Dew and the Dawn."[3] He is not represented as having given grain to the Zuñi by a single and simple act of creation, as did Pi-an-két-tă-chŏl-lă at Taos, but the people had much to do in the first ceremony which gave them the staple Indian cereal. But after they had gone through the long rites, "out from the East-land came Paí-ya-tu-ma" and "touched the plants with the refreshing breath of his flute."[4] Then, as the morning mists cleared away, he, too, disappeared, and was seen but once again, when the people became dissatisfied with the way in which the corn custom was observed. He was sought out. He came back and instructed the people in the old custom, and then, "in the gray mists of the morning, Pai-ya-tu-ma was hidden — and is seen no more of men."[5] The Zuñi " Po-shai-yan-k'ya, the wisest of wise men and the foremost," both in his name and in his qualities, shows similarity to the Sia hero Po-shai-yän-ne, but in that part of the Zuñi myths which Mr. Cushing has thus far published Paí-ya-tu-ma more closely resembles the Sia god.

Before the Taos people were living where they now are, other pueblo people lived in the valley. Traces of what are supposed to have been their houses may still be seen. While these people were living

[1] Eleventh Annual Report, Bureau of Ethnology, pp. 59-67.
[2] Thirteenth Annual Report, Bureau of Ethnology, p. 381.
[3] Ibid., p. 377.   [4] Ibid., p. 395.   [5] Ibid., p. 447.

SOUTH HOUSE, PUEBLO OF TAOS. LOOKING EAST

NORTH HOUSE, PUEBLO OF TAOS. LOOKING NORTH

here, there came a big man, tall as a pine tree, and killed many of
them. Those who were left went away. This giant could drink out
of the Rio Grande by putting one foot on each side of the river,
stooping down and resting his hands on the banks, although the river
in the valley flows between high, steep walls. The track of his foot,
which was left in the rock before it hardened, is about three feet long
and one foot wide. This is up in the hills, not far from the pueblo, and
is said to be covered up now by rain waṣh. The giant had a boy who
used to go around with him, and he, too, left his track on a rock. That
of the man I have not seen, though I have no doubt there exists something which much resembles a man's track, whatever it may be. The
boy's track my friend promised to show me, so we went up to the hills
one day, carrying a small rope, that we might bring down a load of
wood, and so conceal the real purpose of our walk. The impression in
the rock appears to be that of a man's left foot. It is about a foot
long and four or five inches wide. After I had examined it, we scattered sand over it, so that it would not appear that anyone had been
looking at it. The giant and the boy were at last killed by Pi-an-kĕt-
tă-chŏl-lă.

The Sia, too, were troubled by giants. They were called the Skoyo
and were born of the Sia women while the men were away from them
for three years. They ate the people, catching them just as the coyote
catches his prey, then roasting them and eating them. A virgin became
by the Sun-father the mother of twin boys, Máasewe and U'yuuyewe.
One day they went to visit their father, the sun, and he gave them
bows and arrows and three sticks apiece. They then destroyed all the
giants who were eating the Sia people, and, finally, after performing
many great deeds, went back to the Sun-father. He sent them into
the Sandia mountains to live, and there they still live, for their footprints are to be seen on the mountains.[1]

The twin boys in the Sia myth do a part of the work which was
done at Taos by the hero Pi-an-kĕt-tă-chŏl-lă. For the boys destroy
the giants and teach the people some things, such as organization of
the cult societies. But other things which were taught by Pi-an-kĕt-
tă-chŏl-lă to the Taos people, Po-shai-yän-ne taught the Sia.

In the Navajo cosmogony, as given by Mr. Stevenson, are mentioned
two wonderful boys who went to visit their father, the sun. He gave
them bows, arrows, knives, good leggings, and even lightning. With

[1] Eleventh Annual Report, Bureau of Ethnology, pp. 42-57.

their weapons they then killed their enemies and went to live in the mountains. Before leaving they taught the Navajo people songs and prayers.[1] This closely resembles the Sia myth, and probably was borrowed from the Pueblos.

Brinton mentions that among the Muyscas on the Andean plateau the knowledge of their various arts was "attributed to the instructions of a wise stranger who dwelt among them many cycles before the arrival of the Spaniards. . . . his footprints on the solid rock were reverently pointed out long after the conquest."[2] Here it is the culture-hero whose tracks are seen in the rocks, and not those of the giants who ate the people. This is not strange, as these tracks, which so closely resemble the impression of a very large man's foot, might easily be associated either with the culture-hero or with the evil being to whom he is so often opposed.

It is evident that too little of the mythology of the Pueblos, excepting Zuñi and Sia, has been collected to permit an attempt at interpretation yet. I think there can be no doubt that there is at Taos a rich store of mythical lore; this which I have given is certainly the merest beginning.

If we are to follow Mr. Brinton in his interpretation, we have in these culture-hero stories simply sun myths. The wonderful man who teaches the people how to plant, to hunt, and to do all kinds of work, and who brings dry land out of the waters, is only the sun, which makes everything grow, which dries up the waters, and is itself necessary to man's existence. "The story of the virgin mother points, in America as it did in the old world, to the notion of the dawn bringing forth the sun."[3] The hero may go away or be conquered, but he is not killed. So "the sun shall rise again in undiminished glory, and he lives, though absent."[4]

[1] Eighth Annual Report, Bureau of Ethnology, p. 280.

[2] D. G. Brinton, *American Hero-Myths*, pp. 220-21.

[3] *Ibid.*, p. 34.　　　　　　　　　　　　[4] *Ibid.*, p. 30.